© Adam Strickson

An Indian Rug Surprised By Snow

Copyright © Adam Strickson 2005

First Edition

ISBN 1-903110-25-4

Cover Design by Jake Lever

Published in 2005 by
Wrecking Ball Press
24 Cavendish Square, Hull, HU3 1SS

Acknowledgements

To those people who influenced or creatively criticised this poetry: Peter Kiddle, Peter Sansom, Julia Deakin, Susan Burns, James Nash and, for the editing of this collection, Shane Rhodes.

Thanks are due to the editors and directors of the following, where some of these poems appeared in their original form: **Acumen, Staple, Moving Worlds, Envoi, Landscape and Art, Bretton Bermuda, Stories in a Suitcase** (Kirklees Metropolitan Council), **The Oldham Coliseum/Peshkar Productions** programme for 'The Beautiful Violin' and **www.movingstories.org.uk**

Special thanks to Lee Corner at CIDA (Creative Industries Development Agency) and Arts Council Yorkshire, who made this publication possible.

Don't be tempted by the shiny apple
Don't you eat of the bitter fruit
Hunger only for a taste of justice
Hunger only for a world of truth
'Cos all that you have is your soul

From 'Telling Stories', Tracy Chapman

For my mother and father, Kim, Emily, Holly and all the friends within these pages.

Contents

Where are we?..11

British Asians
Green fingers...15
Ramadan 17
Eid Talk 18
The lotus of Safeera awakes and awakes 20
Kabbadi men, 1975 22

Stories from Sonar Bangla (Golden Bangladesh)
A feeling for finches 25
Unexpected conversation with a god 29
The Beautiful Violin 30
The water carriers 32

Early Life
Through the pipe..35
Smoke in the choir 36
Finally water 38
The clever friends 39
Stratford biology 40

Family life
Poem for an outwardly conventional
daughter's 13th birthday..43
The gift 47
Letter to Emily 48
A love of great purity 50

Ancestors real and imagined
Tom Sibley..55
Adam Stirkson of Malhamdale speaks
his diary: 30th March 1002. 57
Notes/glossary for 'Adam Stirkson of Malhamdale'............59
Suddenly in a Lincolnshire Swamp, 317 BC 60

Three houses and a van
We bought it for the view 63
The creature of the black lagoon 64
'Ashfield'..65
K535 HKY – for sale...66

Art and Artists
Vincent and I discuss 'Bedroom at Arles' (Version 3)..........69
Oil on oak 71
Tempera on canvas 72
Masuryas..74
Simon and me 76
Bad cider 77
Satchmo...78
Sidney Bechet 79
Joseph Shabalala explains his music 80

Kurdish Pieces
Below Heptonstall..83
The white home...85
Lost Man 86
For Hulya (in memoriam)..87

Other people, other lives
7 91
Walk/talk/mountain 92
On the train near the farm where Joseph Bramah,
pioneer of hydraulic engineering, grew up..........................97
Wife 98
Teenage son 99
999 100
Five boards waiting 102

Where are we?

Asia is far off. Bin day is here.
The shy bush creatures we call cats
squirt their last marks of the night.
Jammed together gutters leak,
drenching the bleached gnome,
the cut-right-down mint of late October.

Asia is here.
It's been pushed through the bristly letterbox:
the glossy guide to this week's Safeway offers –
lamb karahi with basmati rice
encapsulated in plastic.
Wash it down with Pinot Noir.
The vineyards on our street are not doing well.
Neither is my one piece of washing:
an Indian rug surprised by snow.

Oh, Asia is here again:
the soggy, sodden cotton
barely held by white plastic pegs.
It does not talk the same language
as its neighbour – Clematis Montana.
White plastic is the same colour as fresh snow.
The fingers of the rug maker
have not visited the Himalayas.
More likely they remain busy
in a dark hut in a flat village,
waiting for the driver of the painted lorry.
The driver has Aids.
He is away from home too much.

Once the cows nuzzled
the windows of our houses.
There were no back doors
signalling harsh winds,
thick walls, no deeds,
a poor living.

Asia is far off.
The rug maker is aged
nine and three quarters.

British Asians

Green fingers
Burnley, 2001

The taxi driver slumps in the back of his dented Astra.
If the short haired boys see him, they will kill him.

Stoneyholme. A place of stones flung. Home.
Back-to-backs. Burnley blasted clean of the mill black.

The long radishes have been boarded up
inside the grocers' shops.

The lush strings of Bollywood crescendo
behind the shut-out-the-daylight curtains.

Youths in topis shift in packs, sharing smokes.
A dark blue warrior of the state adjusts his shield.

Once we moved through these mute, sawn off streets
with chanting children, giving gifts of flowers.

We thought hanging baskets would cheer up walls.
After all, the one white couple persisted,
trailing fuchsias among yellow marigolds
above the smearless shine of their window.

Taxi drivers and black haired children came,
prodded compost into baskets,
gently covered the unravelled braids of roots
while women with frayed scarves poured water,
made tea.

The computer room of the Welfare Association
with its proud posters of wide rivers and new bridges
smelt of moist soil and the first monsoon rains
spilling on uncle's yard, half a world away.

We jigsawed a paradise of shapes from thin ply
and painted them the colour of hot rickshaws–
storks, tigers, a shapla flower, a robin, a kingfisher;
a narrowboat rose and castle for the white couple.

We varnished their brightness against the Lancashire wind,
screwed them to sharpened sticks of red stained wood,
and stuck them in boxes and tubs of foliage and buds.

Then we paraded with flute and drum,
carrying a step ladder. We climbed up
and embroidered the doorways and windowsills.

We should have known that colour is not welcome,
that even then some fungoid growth was starting up
outside the boarded up shops of a brick estate
in another neighbourhood, another town.

Ramadan

In the living room of a semi on Eton Avenue,
the two month war flaps,
beating its wings against the walls.

There are no curtains on the windows.
Ahad will buy a length of velvet.
Malik the builder's sister will make curtains.

The garage has gone since my last visit.
Ahad rocks his spoilt son in the cradle.
He believes in the garden, in Adam and Eve.
Mother spreads out her prayer mat on the landing.
Father lies on his bed, felled by back pain:
he would like to plant an apple tree
in the space left by the garage.

The sun goes down. We sit.
We try to understand how flesh ends up in trees.
After prayers, mother spreads a cloth on the carpet.
We eat rice and brussels sprouts with our right hands.
We balance water on the backs of our left hands.
Ahad tells me we could collide with Mars.

In the mountains, on TV,
soldiers mend tyres on jeeps;
wind billows inside the burkahs;
musicians dig up their drums.

It's dark outside. We talk about prophets
before we go to the shop for a pirate DVD.
'Ashoka': a black haired girl in the water,
a white horse, love songs, slaughter
and, in the end, the beginning of a journey,
the end of a war. Red and trees.

Driving home, over the county border:
full beam and half beam in the fog.
A sheep upended with a torn throat.

In the village over the hill - a tyre fitters
and a street festooned with coloured stars.

Eid Talk

Under the dado rail, by the inefficient gas fire,
we talked of war, pretty ankles and 'brush fire':
the sweep of bullets which riddled villagers hiding in the pond.
The family barber paid with his life under the water hyacinth
because he was the family barber.

We ate coconut pancakes. We drank sweet tea.

We talked of great singers and great drunks,
of liberation leaders who'd risk everything for a pretty ankle.
We talked of war, of bloated bodies seen from a rickshaw.
'Don't look! Don't look!'... but the curious child always looks.

We ate coconut pancakes. We drank sweet tea.

Shopon said, 'I had an unusual childhood shooting birds.
Then at St. Mary's, the English school, we were given rifles.
I shot the target, the toilet can we used for ablutions, first time'.
'Get him to the border', they said. 'We need him'.

Instead, his father moved the family from village to village.
Shopon sung harvest songs for the first time, learnt some dances
and the names of four different kinds of rice. He saw more bodies.

We finished the coconut pancakes.

We talked of the exhausted arrival in Dhaka
in time for the night when all the intellectuals were shot.
He told us how the soldier from Baluchistan spared them,
leaving him to spend his adolescence in a land full of ghosts:
machete deaths in horse sheds, witnesses - tongues cut out.

We talked of growing up in England at this time:
the country dances, the butcher with his own slaughter yard.

We asked for more sweet tea.

We discussed electric chairs and the homing habits of toads;
the effectiveness of tiger traps for spiking enemies on bamboo;
the cut off private parts of Pak soldiers on sale in the cattle market.
We talked of Nazrul, the tea boy, national hero, loved for being
a flawed man who could write of Allah and pretty ankles.

We drank more tea.

We talked of a child's war where clichés are real:
'no birds sing/ your sister raped/ your mother killed' -
of how images of war in the magazines of Cotswold Sundays
were true for Shopon, glancing from a rickshaw in East Pakistan.
Then we went quiet, enjoyed sliced mangos and cream.

We talked of truckloads of bodies tipped over the bridge,
of the laka fish which eats human flesh and must not be eaten.

We enjoyed second helpings of mangos and cream.

We talked of animal tracks, snow on the moor and sunsets.

The lotus of Safeera awakes and awakes

She was the child everyone knew,
the child who grew smiles in pots.

She was the child who cooked for everyone,
who already knew a spicy dish of tuna,
prepared with joy, red chilli and cumin,
was a kind of poem.

At twelve, she day dreamed by the radio,
listened to songs of hearts broken in two:
her Dad's 'golden oldies', new as the moon.

At fifteen, she was the school's 'agony aunt',
anonymously answering tear splashed scrawls
with her first poems, which were lovingly stirred
casseroles of emotion.

She spent her nights wrapped in filmi stories:
she looked out on a sky of lotus pollen stars
and wrote and wrote of hearts in pieces.

*

One evening, she heard a DJ on the radio,
fell in love with his sweet mango juice voice
and visited him, every day, in his grocery shop,
where they talked of nothing else but poetry.

She brought him chappatis, cauliflower cheese,
chicken with coriander and mustard leaves:
He said, 'If you cook like this, I'll marry you'.
She said, 'One and one is one, my beloved.'

They moved to the next town but one:
for a year, there was no dirt on the moon's face.
She wrote of a lotus flower opening in the sun.

Then the moon fell out of the sky: she met a crab
who crawled inside her stomach, and sucked her dry.
Her hero left to find a second wife in another land
of deserts and wheat, turning her heart to stone.

He walled her up in their house to cry.
She gave him gold to buy a window stacked high
with ghazals, Hindi themes and Bombay dreams.

He came back to sell the sighs of love to passers-by.
and she wrote, 'One and one is two. I'm bitter inside.'

Their story ended.

*

Then one day she found the moon at her feet,
wiped it clean with the edge of her sleeve,
and threw it up into a sky of pastel pinks.

She logged on and found a chat room guy,
passionate about Urdu lyrics of lovelorn lives.

She painted her nails a screaming peacock blue
and embroidered her new life with sequins.

Kabbadi men, 1975

We leave shoes and mill dust at the fence.
We dip our flared hems in the wet grass.

The sky's grey haired, the sun a dull wax:
we circle-gather as we do round a first car.

A pair of us shuttle backwards and forwards,
push with thin arms – spindles, rods.

Surrounded by sparrows, we fight in turn.
For a clammy hour, we hold each other close.

Our hands are machine nicked, stiffened by work:
we see welding stars in front of our eyes.

Our eyebrows trap the salt of leftover strength.
We pull-crack our knuckles, curse like the English.

A downpour rains off the spice of brotherhood.
We dash for the railings, flap drip-dry sleeves.

The crinkled lines on our white soles are maps.
The damp tongues of our shoes are silence.

Stories from Sonar Bangla (Golden Bangladesh)

A feeling for finches
Directing theatre in Bangladesh

He wakes, fully clothed,
as the plane lands, eleven hours away;
travels by slow buses to Patenga:
a patch of earth under jack fruit trees -
a green glade close to a red brick road
where rickshaws show off
peacocks, butterflies, paper cut stars,
lobsters and loving pairs of birds.

What does he bring?
A diary. Chinese exercises.
A feeling for finches,
The ability to read a place.
A love of sea water.

This is only a beginning. He tells the village:
'Your theatre is your hearths, paths, yards,
fruit trees, boats, net mending sites, lives.
Whatever you have to say, say it loud
with colour, dances, rhythm, emotion
shaped. Whatever you have to say, say it loud
with beauty, with dirt firmly clinging to its roots.'

*

The first exercise: the small dance, flow.

Draw a chalk circle on the dry ground.
Place a group of children inside.
Ask them to stay quiet, internal.
Ask them to close their eyes.
Ask them to feel the sea:
the real sea half a mile from the village
at the end of the red brick road
where nothing grows except
a few transparent shrimps, a water snake;
where meagre catches slither in the bottoms
of their fathers' and uncles' adze hewn boats;

where factory ships and tankers
loom on the horizon of the fish-empty sea
which tosses lives overboard
and sweeps over green glades in cyclones.

Stay quiet, internal, feel the sea.

This is only a beginning. The children rock,
shift weight from foot to foot, alive
to the small dance of water in their bones.
Their hands shape waves, caress the air
like wedding silk.

*

The second exercise: making the beautiful object.

Gather a pile of what's around you – flotsam,
bleached grass, torn blue plastic, palm leaves.
Using pliable cane, weave a tear shaped bowl.
Entwine with foliage, and plastic. Trim.
Thread silver scraps in and out.
Let the ends of the knots dangle.
Wind white cloth around the rim.
Tie in a generous fan of dry palms, like a bird's tail.
Seen from above, your woven bowl will have
the uneven shape of an English lime leaf.

*

The third exercise: transformation of the object.

Ask one girl, thin as a Pennine finch,
to pick up her object and stand in the circle.
A hook of oiled hair flops over her right eyebrow.
Ask her to close her eyes. She is attentive
to the fantailed bowl in her spread fingers.
She feels the sea. The cane ribs rock
and become a boat.

This is only a beginning. She opens her eyes.
An audience steals through the trees:
mothers, old men, the Hindu priest, babies.
For an hour, stooped under low branches,
they watch the beautiful object rock and sail,
shape shifting in the hands of the finch girl.
She drops to one knee:
the bowl becomes a nest, a newborn.
The tail flutters as clouds race through her fingers.
Gripped tight, the bowl becomes an oar.
Lightly held, a flute, a two stringed lute.
A meeting of bleached grass.
Dance and mind in one time:
a storm, a flow of tides, a drowning,
a shoal, a good catch, a heavy boat.

The people who watch, so many now,
crowding the trees, whisper
'This is our lives. This is the good life'

*

For three weeks, he works
among the fruit trees, yards,
on the beach, at net mending sites.
Then the village of Patenga says it loud
with colour, dances, rhythm, emotion
shaped. He invites the newspapers.

In a few short years, the wooden boats
will be hacked to pieces for firewood,
thrown on a pyre of Whitby cobbles
and the Newlyn herring fleet:
The North South breaking of keels,
bonfires on the sands –
the end of the inshore catch.

Back in England, he built ships of willow,
gilded them with gold, rigged square sails –
May ships, winter ships, longboats
which sailed on the seas of terraced streets.
He set loose the black horses.

In Bangladesh, a girl thin as a finch
stands in a chalk circle
and sails a fantailed bowl.

*

An ancient exercise: trance puja.

Each year, at the end of the six seasons,
the grandfathers of the children of Patenga
stuck a felled tree in the pond,
took ropes of plaited creepers
and fixed them at the top of the trunk.
Then, watched by kingfishers, taunting death,
they hung from the ropes' ends,
held by hooks passing through their ears.
They spun round and round,
maypoling the water tree.
They cast out the old, brought in the new.

Unexpected conversation with a god

'Be a human', the boy sings
next to the poet's marble tomb.
Bauls - long hairs, hash smokers -
sing of light and darkness, the one God.
They sing to me. Then the lights go.
We leave in darkness,
wrapped flowers slipped into our hands.

We walk on a road of ghosts.
'This is a temple', says Shaheen
of the lazy eye, 'built by a cotton king'.
The iron gate sings.
Darkness, darkness – lit by two candles.
Adjusting our eyes we see them:
gods behind bars with amputated arms.

Ganesh, the chipped, glittering elephant-god
leans against a grave, rubbing his swollen belly.
His fat kindness looks me straight in the eye, says:
'I may be clumsy but I'll twist out of these bars.
I'll loose the monkeys chained in the street of garments.
I'll find a tree for Jinna's squirrel, unchain the parrots.'

I tell him I'm sad about the animals.

'Shipping, shipping', says Ganesh,
'I hate to see the darkness of their bright colours.
These humans shove them from port to port,
keep them down in dark, dark holds,
force them to eat their own shit in wicker cages.
I'll open the lids, free the snakes, let the birds fly.'

Shaheen leads us out past more graves –
Hindu humans buried sitting down.
Darkness, darkness – the smell of rice straw.
Later we are shown photos of raped women,
smashed buildings, shot men: the invasion.

The Vice Chairman talks of Ilford, Essex;
Brighton beach, light and darkness.
Bauls sing for everyone, ask me for money.

The Beautiful Violin

In a wood, alone, naked, Bhelua dances.
In her head a violin is playing.
The line of her waist curves.
Hidden by trees, Amir sees her, thinks
'A slender neck, skin smooth as wood:
This woman is like a violin

which sings in my skin, a violin
which plays for me. Her dances
fiddle the feet, set fire to wood
which heats my blood. She is playing
a girl in love with love', thinks
Amir as the lilt of her curves

dips and curls until the dance of her curves
stops when she hears a twig break. The violin
in her head freezes. She thinks
'Who's there? Who watches my dances?
Are there children playing
hide and seek in the wood?'

Amir stands still as a block of wood
but she cries out as she spies the curves
of his bow behind a branch. 'He's not playing
but hunting and I'm the prey, a violin
he wants to play as he dances
between my thighs.' Bhelua panics, thinks

'He's seen me naked.' Amir thinks
'She knows I'm here. I'll run from the wood
before I snap the strings of the violin who dances
for herself alone, the beautiful violin whose curves
light fires on my skin.' Amir runs but the violin
of the dance curves in his head. She's playing

his blood faster and faster, her fingers playing
all over his skin. 'Only love', he thinks,
'can play like this.' He turns back to see the violin
of breasts, of waist, of thighs. He runs through the wood
to meet her eyes. His hands run over her curves
and her skin dances and his skin dances

a jig of love playing the million leaves of the wood
so that Bhelua thinks and Amir thinks their curves
are playing like one violin as all around the wood dances.

The water carriers

They said the dew some summers fills the bowls
and round, turned earth sings to the slurp of cows.
They said sometimes the sea fog brews up
and sends a tower, stacked with pots of rain:
Frogs leap twigs, hurdle furrows, skitter clefts
and rush to spawn where now the grass tufts dry.

I told them I'd seen a river of sand
where, in a gully, three men ribbed a boat
they'd never sail – one day cut up for roofs.

They said this place is a pitcher of hills
where children have always dipped their fingers
in circles made to catch a yolk of moon.

I told them I'd seen a woman of bones
who carried months of water on her head
and took an hour to cross the river bed.
A man had built a hut half way across:
He squatted by a fire, kneading cakes
of rice, molasses, dates. He sold me one
which tasted of dung smoke and short lives.

Early life

Through the pipe

Bitsy and Keith and Guy had already done the dare.
They'd done it like men on tractors – quickly, gruffly.

Now he had to go, the wimp, the weed. *Easy*, they said,
to duck down, crawl through, come out the other side.

I'll run back home, he said inside, but the dare was ice
gripped in his fist which wouldn't melt, a gottadoitnow.

He slithered through thin water, litter, a snaggle of twigs,
banged his head, grazed his knees and stopped dead.

Bitsy jumped down, jabbed him with a snapped branch:
that got him moving, though he whimpered and whined.

He made it to the other side, wet wellied and bloody.
They'd scarpered, nicked off for penny chews and bubbly.

He ran all the way home, snivelled past 'Batman's Leap',
where he'd once jumped from bank to bank, with eyes shut.

His mother swabbed his gritty knees, sat him on her lap,
asked him which school friends he wanted at his party.

In his tent of bedclothes, he made up the story of a pipe
with no one at the beginning, no one at the end,
just a boy in disguise, and light at the end of darkness,
the other side of a dare.

Smoke in the choir

Treble   Surplices   Burn

and memory comes to my eyes:
two thirds of a wooden saint
hundreds of years old, one shouldered,
torn from the organ loft by the church warden.

The choirmaster said: 'I've brought her home.
Old Edmonds had already fed one to the boiler.
The church was cold. Cecilia was next.'

He stroked the saw tooth marks,
sanded down her rough places,
counted the keys on her organ.
His wife polished her long gown.
His son looked into her eyes.

She sat in the different rooms of childhood.
Her fingers, smooth as wax tapers, played solemn sounds
in the dead hours between school and tea.
The boy finger-nailed the dust between the pipes.
The choirmaster told him she was the patron saint of music.

The boy found out more.
They tried to roast her to death in a dry bath.
She reclined there coolly for three days.
Then they hacked her head off.

She played the organ, like the choirmaster,
She sang, like the boy.
Her voice was the most beautiful of things.
Angels came to sing around the bath.

Some things the boy left disappear for ever
like his *treble* voice,
like sap stains left by daffodils
pinned to *surplices*   on Easter morning
and some remain, like Cecilia, like *burn*.
She was the most beautiful of things. She is.

Angels   Voice   Burn

and memory comes to my eyes:
a photo of children in striped pyjamas.
They could have been choirboys, choirgirls.
They stand in the back of a lorry.

Soon after, they are shovelled on a fire.

Most beautiful of things, the human voice,
stops. They become black smoke,
then absent, disappeared
like Cecilia's shoulder.

Finally water

Far, far back she was new: spray fresh cactus green,
a Commer Auto-sleeper with orange curtains primed
for adventure. Father, the adventurer, couldn't wait.

When holiday July comes, fly out to mainland Europe.
Look around. She must be there, somewhere.
She was always there. You can't miss cactus green,
two English boys, the younger one with ginger hair.

She's there, proud in a field on the Czech border
next to the barn with horse sleighs waiting for winter,
near the wood where the boys find the haunted shovel.

Cross the Alps to Rome, she's there, St. Peter's Square.
Quiet! The elder brother's asleep behind the curtains.
He sleeps all morning, never visits St. Peter's.

Go to Austria. She's there. Cactus green
next to the log café which serves chips and table football.
Mother drinks rum and Coke. The boys drink Fanta.
The adventurer drinks, devours guide books, German novels.

In the forest the boys see a hoopoe. Go there.
Walk along the path: there's the hoopoe!
Oh, the sun has set. Forked lightning. The boys play Snap.

It's morning – they tickle each other, open the side door,
stick their heads out, breathe in the lake.
A whole week at a campsite! Who's that over there?
Two pretty German sisters from Essen in matching bikinis.
Maybe the girls play table football, drink Fanta, maybe they'll say hello.
Maybe the boys won't go to a church or a museum or stay in a coal yard
for a whole week. Maybe
they'll swim.

The clever friends

My photo shows you, hairless and quietly sunny,
with your hands on the shoulders of your son, Adam,
who has the face of a yellow elephant with one tusk -
more than enough to conjure the cliché, 'Truth is...'

The truth is the elephant's a mask from the cellar
and, after the thirty year gap, you look like your father,
not the boy better than me at maths, the other misfit
who knew how to bowl overarm and catch rabbits.

For you, my cellar was not a surprise but a memory
of how I always liked to make things: 3D scenes
culled from the National Geographic – a Mongolian yurt,
an Amazon hut on stilts with poster blue flowing below.

I was not so good at science and had forgotten how,
when asked to find some 'dense material' from home
to be sunk or weighed, I brought a scrap of corduroy,
not a piece of Honiton stone or a six inch nail.

Truth is I was always a piece of dense material,
incapable of 'verbal reasoning' or the logical steps
which took you to the infrastructure of new technology
and a detailed knowledge of the rugby world cup.

You live among the straight lines of the south
while I'm stuck in this higgledy-piggledy world
of weaving snickets, ginnels and back-to-backs,
where I thought I'd learnt to disappear the past.

Truth is it's here, in the room of the photo, with us,
though you say we should go back to the village,
walk about, call in at the forbidden 'Red Lion',
go up the Donkey Fields and find a slower time.

Truth is I grew up, helped to make a Kyrghiz yurt
and sat in a hut on stilts over a mosquito river.
You explored Australia in a four-wheel drive
and may settle there with your palm-top sons.

Truth is it's Saturday: on top of Windmill Hill, I can see
two black spots who have just found a carthorse shoe.

Stratford biology

You found them in the backroom, sent to wash out a pipette.

You knew those two addled, pickled eggs with webbed hands,
sealed in brown glass, were two might-have-been-children,
who guarded between them, a skull, a dirty thing with teeth.

They sat, eating their own tails, on the shelves above
owl pellets, claws, carapaces, winged bones and eyeballs.

You knew this flesh and bone was out of place, vaguely illegal.

You stared at the folded crinkles of two underwater cheeses,
worried by their closed eyes, unconvinced by their quietness.
You tipped the edge of one jar, watched the still life judder
and failed to connect it with a cloudy act under a car blanket
by someone in gingham, and someone in winklepickers.

You found the skull easier, closer to sketched rabbit bones
with its cracks like grubby fingernails and hard after-life.

You picked it up like a fumbling Dad with his newborn
and pushed aside the sniggered whisper of, 'Alas...'
with 'Blest be he that spares these bones', engraved
beneath Shakespeare's stone belly in the church:
the verger told you his bones had gone down river,
washed out by floods slip-slapping the chancel floor.

You looked up at the two unswimming whitenesses,
thought of the weighty burgher, slumped over his desk,
dying, crying for his lost son, Hamnet, twin brother of Judith,
but couldn't give names to lives without birth, without death.

Family life

Poem for an outwardly conventional daughter's 13th birthday.

Your name is Holly Ravinder.
Learn to like it.
Call yourself Princess of the Sun,
Little Running Glen or
Holly Red Berry.
Let people laugh at you.

Continue to relish
a thousand shades
of nail varnish.

Know that your scars are beautiful,
whether from chicken pox, a boat hook
or scrambling up the Kashmiri foothills.

Do not cough up the dust of libraries
but enjoy damp books
especially thin volumes of poetry
dried in the sun like razor fish
which smell of salt and rock pools.

Make pegs from hazel twigs
and sliced baked bean tins.
Know what chitties are
and relish the flavour of field mushrooms
cooked over a smoky campfire.

Remember that Macdonalds use only three varieties
of green salad worldwide.
Grow fifteen, including Haitian spinach
on a hidden patch by the motorway.
Fry them with tamari and a stolen goose egg.

Do not hunt for a career.
Hunt for British butterflies without nets
including the small brown on the cliff paths of the Isle of Wight.

Do not buy clothes from 'Sportsmania'
or any other breeze block ugly
discount warehouse on the edge of a city.

Once a year
paint yourself green
not any green
but a thick oily viridian
and stick on some leaves.
You can dye your pubic hair
a burnished copper.

Drum through the night – monthly.

Smell a bit –
the smell that you get when you only wash
with cold water from a stream once every three days
but enjoy hot springs and Turkish baths
when you have the chance.
See yourself as a female Gandhi
but not to the extent of denying yourself sex
or pomegranates.
Wear purple saris.
Sing like Bessie Smith.
Marry no-one but become expert in
the Tantric arts of love
and non-violent direct action.

Keep fit with a yet undiscovered
Amazonian martial art
which can be performed
only to the sound of rocks
knocked together.

Sit quietly on the tarmac
before riot shields
and let yourself be dragged away –
at least you were there.

Always be aware of the full moon.

Become a scientist in a shed –
discover a theory
and get a famous writer called Bill or Joan
to name it after a goddess.

Live simply
but remember breakfast can be
croissants with butter from a Jersey cow
between sips of freshly brewed real coffee.

Adore Beckmann, Proust
and Theravada scriptures.

Love one person all your life
flagrantly and secretly.

Salsa in the street.

Listen to the lyrics of
Bob Dylan, Elvis Costello and Heinrich Heine.

Borrow a telescope
and learn the names of the stars.

Read The Iliad, Tales of Ovid
and Kerouac's 'On the Road'.

Live in a tent.
Enjoy conversations about Armenian music, the Gnostics of Provence
and the genetic reasons for the colouring of the goldcrest.

When you're really depressed,
try half a bottle of Jack Daniel's Tennessee whisky
or a swim.

Walk, travel by wooden boat,
horse, rickshaw, mule or dray.
In winter, find places where
snow shoes are essential.

Do not live to be 130
but live long enough to be wise and old.
Pay no pension contributions and do not be a
a stakeholder in anything offered
through the post or telesales.

Let no man tell you what to do –
especially your dad.

The gift

At two you wore a pink coat with a twig in your hand.
At three you were Gerda searching for frozen Kay.
At four you were the princess of camels,
dancing in the desert of the sitting room.
At five you were 'thirsty as a mole.'
At six you looked forward to piano lessons
and your little sister was 'driving you ships.'
At seven we stopped keeping notes.
At eight you told us, 'God says no fighting'
as you stood between us in the kitchen.

At seventeen, in a black dress,
on the eve of your birthday,
you sing about a silver swan.

This October a thousand Hooper swans
leave Iceland and fly over glaciers
to winter in the reed beds of Lancashire.

Because you never really want anything,
we give you a silver watch
to remind you of swan time
and because unhurried time
is what you have always given us.

One day you will find Kay in the ice palace.
A camel will take you into the sand dunes.
You will have a special baby named Blossom.
God will visit you in his dressing gown.

You already have thirty pairs of shoes.

You will fly like the swans
and return each winter.

Letter to Emily

I

It has to begin. With you, we began with toys:
two gods in a swinging seat, a monkey drum,
packets of bangles, dolls from each far off place
I visited – as if you were a sailor's child.
And you were always one journey behind,
living in half stories and jumbled costumes.

Do you remember that birthday party when
your little friends were asked to take a trail
from room to room? They had to find the countries
on shelves, on walls, on doors, and hung from lights.
They were amazed at our bazaar, at how
a terraced house becomes the coloured world.

But you know it's not just the trinket stalls.
You've seen the boards which hide the holes
where windows used to be, been called *good girl*
by Sikhs surprised at *please* in the corner shop.
You tried to tell the girls at school that *Paki*
is not a word which easily makes friends.

You wore shalwaar kameez for Bernie's show:
Just like 'The King and I', she said, not knowing
we'd bought it ten minutes away by bus.
You got to know our friends, like Apu, Pav,
Shanaz, Kali, Sazzad – and made your own:
Odsi, and Mamsi who calls me *Mister Dad*.

II

It has to begin. For me, it was my mother
reading a story: *'Epaminondas'*, a boy
with curls, a mischievous snotty picanin,
black as the suck-tube of a sherbet-dab.
And then a sitar on the radio sang
and floated me to an Indian afternoon.

Later on, my turn to tell the stories
in draughty halls behind those sooty walls
with under fives whose Bradford mums and dads
had come from mountains, plains and bushy hills.
We whispered all our words for grass and green,
found out our names were saints and prophets.

We turned the globe and spun the coloured world,
discovered towns which melted in the mouth:
Peshawar, Sylhet, Lahore, Ahmedabad.
Hasnara, from Bengal, helped out with words,
brought in her bedspread, unfolded for us all
her schoolgirl days of rivers, chickens, rain.

I took a plane to see where she had played,
shared feasts of Coke and biscuits in woven huts.
Then I knew her home was not my home,
that this was bigger still and almost silent:
a plait of leaves; you sing, I sing, we sing.
The rest is gunshot wounds, the Wild West.

A love of great purity

Twenty one years ago, they were moving north.
He'd gone ahead, already swallowed the darkness.

He lived in an engine house, a monument of wind leaks
and piston driven ghosts, among puppeteers and painters
who toiled by flakes of daylight, knocking up a midwinter tale.

Fingers nimble to the beat of Ska, they cut, stuck and soldered
tin stars, sacking camels, the cracked mirror of a unicorn's horn.

He began to dream of blue wolves.

The worst time was waking up, lying there too cold to stir
on the shelf half way up the wall, an audition for the morgue.

He lay in the just after dawn blur, thinking of her, his two year wife,
leaving the sea light of Cornwall for this mill needled valley of snow.

He thought of how she'd look at him and at the crusty curry pans,
the icebergs of milk, the mess left by three days of frozen pipes.

He thought of his friends' eyes staring out from huddles of greatcoats,
their hands in fingerless gloves clutching mugs of tea by the unlit stove.

She'd turn right around or stand there crying for what they'd left behind.

In a moment of enlightenment, he slid down the ladder, found shampoo,
grabbed a lump hammer, knocked over a paint can, unbolted the door.

Outside, there should have been bears.

He stamped round to the dustbin water butt.
He thought of her warm skin, concealed.

He smashed the hammer down onto the ice.
He struck water and plunged his head in.

He pulled out and, with hands like paving stones,
bashed the shampoo into his hair, dipped again.

The sleepers awoke, blearily aware of pain, outside in the snow.
They shuffled out to witness the last soapy drips of his pure act.

Twenty one years on, he meets one of the watchers
who remembers the breaking of ice and her thought -
'Who was this woman who inspired such love, or fear?'
She tells him she knew even then, whatever happened,
whatever bitter islands, he'd always return to the one
who didn't notice his clean hair that twilit afternoon,
who stood in the chaos and let her tears trickle down.

Ancestors real and imagined

Tom Sibley

Something -
Rebecca Charlotte's childbed death at twenty seven?
A pinch of Atlantic salt on his mottled grey duck egg?
A crow's nest tale of harpooning the whale in Arctic sea?
An unwillingness to break his back with heavy sacks?
Something
made the thirteen year old boy run from the flour mill.
Something
made him clog down the lane in his Sunday best.
Something
bailed out fresh water, threshing and grinding stones
for the sky scraping rigging of the majestic Mauritania,
The Last Grain Race, the frothing milky ocean.

He rounded the savage Horn, called in at Chittagong,
circled round the world at least a baker's dozen times.
He met a number of forty foot waves, some strange fish
and even (he told me more than once) ate an albatross.

He was the kind of grandfather a boy should have,
taught me how to use his marlinspike, essential tool
for completing wall and crown, three times round -
The Turk's Head, Neptune of knots.

Voyaging for years, with untold compassion and sacrifice,
petty rivalries, equator crossing antics, meetings with lascars,
month old oranges, honour, pity and dry sand-grit biscuits,
he rose from boy to navigator, from sail to diesel-turbine,
familiar with cleats, chandlers and shipboard obscenities.
He found time to marry above himself (well she thought so)
and to father one daughter south of the Thames, his 'Dolly'.

Thirty years in, he found himself on Cape Town beach
with six Zulu spears in his head.

Coming home (though he never really did)
he entered a bevy of slightly la-dee-dah women,
his wife's sisters, cousins and familiar extensions.
He became a man of less than a few words,
worked casually as a storeman, supervising cardboard.

We shared my grandma's surprise cakes (never a surprise)
'Would you like another one dear? Tom?'
at 329 Battle Road, Hastings,
when Mods and Rockers were current.

On a good day, the rain brought a cargo of salt
though he never took a bus to the bottle glass promenade.
He preferred to send smoke signals from his armchair,
roll Old Holborn incessantly,
imprison his ships in well corked bottles.
He did the old sailor bit with no real energy,
liked TV Wimbledon, an occasional saved-up pee,
the ten minute ritual of stripping a Fox's glacier mint.
He ate slower than a hamster and went to bed early.

Finally
the mill flour burrowed, then became his skin
despite a million and one leagues over the sea.
He shed scales continuously,
scratched his arms until they bled.

Finally
he scratched his wrist, arms, shins, ankles
until they bled and bled and bled
until he fell from the rigging for the first time.

Adam Stirkson of Malhamdale speaks his diary: 30th March 1002.

Four days gone
                since horse-giving.
Knuckles grit raw
                from soil shift.
Thumb grykes
                mud clogged.
Nails thorn sore.
                Even in frost freeze
wondered at fish wings
                in stone haul
and hairy snail
                caught in deep dead.

Enough noddle grub.
                Up with spelk sun
now grown grand.
                Must up over Hanlith
while He who all can
                holds his bladder.

Slack beak heron
                ships over Gordale.
Sling-shot larks
                rise from bog grass
break into feathers
                in sun squint.
Again. Again.
                Ah the day!

I'll strackle hours
                lie on moor bed
loose spine beads
                while sun toasts
mighty neb
                share tattle
with gabby curlew.

Slack back!
    Work bellows
 in barn below.
    I come. I come.

One beast
    not high pastured
 hoofs muck
    tethered to rudster
sick in maw
    withy thin.
I fetch hay
    for mew
fill drenching horn
    with balsam
force gullet
    stroke unders.
Be reet.
    Beasts know me.
Name Stirkson
    son of stirk.
Not for nowt.

Sun's mid-up.
    Lass calls.
Must within walls.
    Back by beck
pick butterbur.
    My own missis.
She'll wash
    this stiff shirt
sit me down
    with curd cake
kuss mi lips.
    Ah the day!

Notes/glossary for 'Adam Stirkson of Malhamdale'

Horse-giving – horses were given at weddings in Saxon times; perhaps Adam Stirkson has given a horse to his daughter's new husband.

Grykes – deep cracks in the limestone, as found in the 'pavement' above Malham Cove.

Noddle – head or brain.

Spelk – splinter.

He who all can – God.

Strackle – to waste (time).

Neb – nose.

Tattle – chatter or gossip as in 'tittle-tattle'.

Slack back – lazy person.

Rudster - post used for tethering cattle in the barn.

Maw – stomach.

Withy – a thin willow branch, harvested to make baskets.

Mew – the manger or eating-trough.

Drenching horn - horn hung in every field barn, used to administer medicine.

Stirk – young cow or bullock.

Butterbur – the butterbur grows by streams; the leaves were used to wrap butter.

Suddenly in a Lincolnshire Swamp, 317 BC

I was watching 'Meet the Ancestors'
when I heard the calling music, knew
I'd stopped there on the long causeway,
looked into the marsh, seen my own eyes
stare back, smelt rubbed lavender
on my muddy palms, brother bloodied.
When Eodric told of the eclipse -
the dull blood on mother moon
and her winter need for the death
of a hard fighter - Sigur made sure,
with gifts of grain and antler handles,
they would raise hands against his wife's ruiner.

They made me sword-mark my brother's back
before he fell forward into the oak logboat,
shoved by Sigur, who had wide-wished
his early end as the moon's gift.
My brother loved to raise metal into shields.
Now he's below the reeds, in the other world.

They drowned the boat, pegged it into the peat.
He lies in it, held down with a stone.
They've sloped off, buried the drums.
The water from my eyes breaks the water.
I do not know the word for 'mirror'
but I am no longer in the same place as my brother.

Three houses and a van

We bought it for the view

Opposite, a church, bearing Christ, well carved,
hammered into the wall in fog.
"Mummy, they're nailing a man to the wall".

Ash trees, two
darken houses like a thunder cloud
growing out of the ground, yanked
up.

On the pavement a camping table.
Leaning, a kerb-breaking of large vans.
Catering. TV faces in nurses' uniforms
looking much older, more tired
than on the small screen.
Looking job ordinary.

Always the programme is not reality
but partial reality – the sentimental,
settee, club friendly village.
Of course there's suffering
but tears are dolls' water.
Auntie doesn't stick her tongue out
at the promising teenager's funeral.

Sometimes cows walk on the roofs,
edging slowly from one house to another.
Sometimes there are fires,
the banging walls of marriages,
a kitchen row at a lantern window
the other side of the garages.

Opposite, in the ditch, crisp packets, freezing.
Litter pick: feel the crack in your hand.
White streaks in the sky: two parallel lines.
Mares' tails pulled and pulled till the whole horse is tail.

The creature of the black lagoon

Another man had lived there for a year
when he came back and climbed the trellis fence,
stood by 'the cove': his pond, a spoon of black,
a garden centre romance, yearned for, once.

He cupped the leather of his camera case.
The fountain gone, just algae thick as jam.
He plunged his hand in deep and cold, felt metal,
hoicked out a firedog, then a knife and fork.
The paving slab still there, on which he'd placed
his chimney oven, and one night, baked apples.
Camera, chimenea, chimera. He took
a photo of an eyeless dog with slimy tail.

He dropped the knife back in, which stuck, like Excalibur,
blade upwards, not sure about going down or coming up.

'Ashfield'

The new house oozes winter,
so we make fire in the basement,
wait for the glister of wet coal.

We lose each other in crannies,
call forlornly from floor to floor,
lost in hundred acre boxes

Electricians punch holes in walls,
leave copper bristles in carpets,
give advice on dying goldfish.

We prise off anaglypta,
look down on coal tits,
build up bottles in the evenings.

Our daughters say the decoration
is like a pudding, so you make two,
glut the kitchen with fruity steam.

We hear stuff: 'Ah, that house:
fifty years, she filled it with paper.'
'There's always been disputes'.

We've mended ours, cover cracks
with polyfilla, sand down,
look up at the ceiling roses.

K535 HKY – for sale

Consider
the shoe-loads of sand swept out of the back
and the few grains which remain -
stubborn clues to Blackpool day trips:
the sleep of sisters among damp towels,
the wet backed eye rub of arrival home.

Remember
this was mainly a work van, used to potholes
and sky emptying reservoirs of rain.
It was a family vehicle on salty days
and one August holiday in northern Denmark.

This is a good buy
despite the dents, the brush marks of new paint,
the soft crisps in the grooves of rubber matting,
the painful failure of marriage guidance
during a six year service history.
The engine is a mountain without end.

Consider this van
as a high waterfall behind which you can hide.

You may enter it as we did Denmark –
not expecting sun – and find yourself
with an easy view over dry-stone walls
on a day of Pennine rainbows.

The twelve tracks on 'Mellow Miles',
which have softened many ridges,
will return to a small collection of jazz.
The matching spanners will stay.

Art and Artists

Vincent and I discuss 'Bedroom at Arles' (Version 3)

Vincent, this picture
is an affirmation of pain.
I can't believe you think
looking at it
rests the brain.

I know
you painted your white chair yellow
to let in sunshine
but why did you hammer three inch nails
into the walls
and block up the window
with those mucky bricks?

When you borrowed money
to buy the bed
you told me
you were going to paint
a child on the headboard
or a nude.
You were going to paint
some company.

No Vincent,
a self portrait is not
company.

I've left some presents
to cheer you up when you get home -
no, not more tubes of thick yellow paste:
Ask your brother for those.

In the blue vase,
I've placed a bouquet of children.

Under the red counterpane,
you'll find a wife.

I left a baguette
and some Belgian chocolate
on the bedside table.

Gaston's coming round tomorrow
to sort out the window.

Oh, I've confiscated your gun –
I found it behind the Japanese print.

I can't work out
why the chair seat
is a lily pad
but when they let you out,
I suggest you fold up
those violet walls of loneliness
and give them to the postman.

What do you mean,
you've run out of paint?
You haven't listened
to a word I've said, have you ?

Do you eat the stuff?

Oil on oak

A green dress, a man's fur collar -
two Italian figures
entwined among furniture,
reflected in a mirror.

Two cold householders,
familiar with linen and scalloped chests.

They savour the upholstered comfort,
the cinnamon of ten years' marriage,
have no unspoken thoughts
or clashing draperies.
The downy forms of green, unripe walnuts
lie on polished boards at their feet.

They close the shutters,
strip in slats of daylight,
make love standing up
as if long separated
by prison or countries.

Outside it is Whitsuntide -
a procession of white banners.

Later, their child
brings them an oak tree in a pot.
The word 'acorn' is important –
it is the colour of the mirror frame
cut like dog's teeth
which hangs above
their linked, long fingered hands.

They live for themselves,
smelling of cake and skin.
They grow old together,
though he is much older than her.

I go out and buy a book
of the world's greatest paintings:
the picture is a marriage certificate.

I did not remember the orange
on the windowsill:
the forbidden fruit.

Tempera on canvas

Switch off the club mix.
Turn off the main road.
Stop. Put the handbrake on.
Take the keys out of the ignition.
Get out of the car.
Lock the door.

Walk through the wood.
Notice the gold tips on the tree trunks
and the single blue anemone.

When you get to the seashore,
take the slides out of your hair.
Undress.

Lay your jacket
decorated with embroidered roses
carefully on the cool green ground.

Put your rings and slides
in a plastic bag
at the base of the bulrushes.

Step into the scallop shell.
Hide your body with your hands.
Imitate the pose of a statue.

You are modest, beautiful and chaste.
The Romans call you Venus.

Don't worry about the tides.
Zephyr, the west wind,
will keep blowing you back to the shore.

Stop giggling. Stand still.
Stop showing off
the pink varnish on your toenails.

Become what you naturally are.
No one is stealing your car.

Masuryas

Masuryas *was the temporary sculpture by*
Anish Kapoor, named after the satyr
who was whipped to death by Apollo,
which took up the entire length
of the Turbine Hall at the Tate Modern in 2002.

I

The kind of red that stains the road
after the wreck's been towed away.
The kind of red that seals a wound
after the surgeon's dumped his gown.

The public know this is just one take.
You can hear their snickered guesses
like *trumpets, potholes, a tunnel of love,*
a slide, a ride, a man's inside, a hide,
a trap, a crazy coffee mill, an inner ear,
something you see after a skinful of beer,
His Master's Voice without the dog, a curve
of fire, a hot desire, a big red thing,
a fart, the Moby-Dick of modern art.

They leave wonder and wet footprints
while huge words sing in the hall of odd
like *meditative, worship, power, God.*

It's easier to talk engineering, the HOW
of bridges and turbines, the great big WOW!
It's easier to talk force, fields of strength,
to describe the three steel rings, the length
of the thing, the welds, the sheer size,
the way the horizontal flies.

But the dark, dark red seeps out.

II

A boy grew up in Bombay, a boy
threw powders at Holi, a boy fell in love
with pigment, a boy grew up with gods:
blue Krishna, the red flames of Durga.
A boy saw taxis turned upside down,
which spilt passengers and blood into dust.

A man who was once a boy
threw himself up into the sky
and landed in white rooms
which he filled with cones
of perfect, blue powder.

Now he has found this dark, dark red,
which invites us to death and prayer.

III

In my room, five views of 'Masuryas' on screen.
Live sound brings clues: hush, a susurration,
the trill of a girl, hush, *huh* of an out-breath.
People move, then go still. When they are still,
they're monochrome. They are light. They shine.

People are present, then they are absent.
They walk up, walk down, walk round, lean down:
in each place there is a circle to which all lines lead;
in each place there are lines which end in circles.
They touch red. They are light. They are gone.

Simon and me

It was the stickers made me think of you:
A cup of char, a red Ferrari car,
a heart, a star, a blue twelve string guitar
and the sticky words – 'MASTER', 'COPY'.
You are. I don't.

We both write round here but you got to stuff
before me: packhorse bridges, old tyres, moors
which spew sheep into streets and doors
I'll never pass because I'm not Huddersfield enough.

Someone told me you're moving to my town,
though places round here are more yours than mine.
Bet it'll be a penthouse flat in Sunnybank Mill
with a window in the roof which lets starlight spill
on your late night mug of Auden, while you down
a good malt.

Bet you like the Chronicle – the darts divisions
and cricket. The stories of all male pantomimes
are part of you - your Dad's in charge - but times
change and incomers are common as pigeons
in these parts. Like me.

Nineteen moves and seven counties after school,
I ended up on your turf. I like it round here:
the rough edges, a daughter who speaks hard
and the grass on West Nab you can swim in.

But last month I cancelled the Chronicle –
Too much subsidence, death and the usual crew;
angling news to sup over down the Social
but I don't go, don't own my own snooker cue.
Bet you do.

Bad cider

Liquor of Pig's Snout,
Laurie Lee's poison,
the hard stuff, the tart scrumpy
which made him lurch out of the pulpit,
the fiddler-diddler of Slad, lover and leaver,
while the half-brewed cherryade child
sat in the church with bated ears
soured by the poet's slurred speech
which read so sweet, so Rosie
on the page.

Satchmo

He grew up in the South
where women went for each other with razors.

He grew up in a swamp of hot, black flies.
He sang like a battered trumpet.

His moon was a desperate, aching blue
a heart-bawling, beaten in the corner, sex-it-up moon
a moon like a punched eye
a moon like a long B flat
lipped down – a big mouthed cry.

He knew how to be-bop hum the honeyest tune
until suits and aprons jumped up and jived.

He died in his den at Corona.
His fourth and longest wife, Lucille,
loosened the latch on the window,
marvelled at the harmony of the All Stars
and the bruised, blue note beauty of the moon's halo.

Sidney Bechet

They let the midwife of the soprano sax out of the lock-up.
A snake of light waited for him, curled round his horn
so he jumped the Channel and committed sexual affray
with Joplin's Maple Leaf Rag.

He shoved a cock between its spindly thighs,
blew slapped handfuls of notes up its arse
until a new scale burst out of its mouth,
headed under the draughty door of the club
and set off for the future.

Once the tune knew who was in charge,
he force marched it along the streets of New Orleans,
threw it in the air like a skating girl
then hollered at the band when they couldn't keep up.

He popped into a tattoo house and burned it on his arms.

A goose hissed as he passed the coop with it.

He'd only bought the odd brass clarinet on a whim.
Now it's the coolest thing, though he was hot for it,
typed a message from hell with his fat fingers,
sweated with the heat of a closed cell.

Joseph Shabalala explains his music*

Snuffles of oxen and my whispers in their ear
started a breathy song in my head, long ago,
before the whoosh of the road, the fear
of trucks, before Ladysmith got too big
and trafficked out the walking sounds.

Back then I was a barefoot boy with a stick.
I buzzed the shacks with clap whoop joy
and called a herd of notes in from the bush.
I hushed my mother to hear the stew bubble
and lullabyed myself with the tin roof scuttle.

In that far away, run in the road childhood,
I talked to the beasts and tickled their chins.
Then I learnt to sing our conversations
about yokes, rope, cruel men, the smell of dust
and in the north, long long ago, Bethlehem.

*Joseph Shabalala is the founder and leader of the South African singing group: **Ladysmith Black Mambazo.**

Kurdish Pieces

Below Heptonstall

Ibo's in a donkey jacket. We're down in the woods
kicking a soggy March of last year's leaf mess.
Twenty of us. The Kurds sing, 'Who let the dogs out?'
They bark. They howl.

The fulling mill pounded out a rhythm in these trees
Clogs from down the valley clayed up before the sun rose
and John Wesley rode in on his mare with her short legs.

Rojgar says it's like a mountain.
Steep. A scramble. He's been there –

'My cousin. He die. Very cold. Very cold.
Policeman follow. Gun. My friend. He die.'
He bleats like a ram lost on a mountain.
Someone barks. Someone howls.

Three of the Kurds join hands, toe leaves.
Ibo holds his scarf above his head like a yawn.
They sing a song about a woman or a massacre.
Someone howls. Someone takes a photograph.
Then they all dance, the seven men marooned
in a wood reserved for dogs and wrapped up children.
They pocket their phones. They step together.

'Join. We show you. Yalla, yalla!'
Ibo is *chop*i – leader. You follow.'
Twenty of us snake through the woods.
The barks stop. The non-joiners join in.

What they told us was quieter than tree trunks:
'We followed the sheep. We hid under trucks.
The dogs came. We were black with diesel.
They locked us up. We came here. You found us.
Look, we are friends. We dance. We sing.'

In these woods, no one follows us.
In this valley, no one shoots at us.

There was some quietness
before we wrecked the playground
with the three men on a swing routine
and the Kurds started to bark again.

The white home

In their house, someone is always in nightclothes.
Old men with moustaches and huge laughs fill the screen.
'Come in, come in, you are welcome. Turkia coffee?'
Cardamom - dark dregs like pigment, like lake silt.

The second honoured guest is above the fireplace:
Oil paint on scrap wood: a woman in a room –
done quickly, his son Juan says, not like a proper painter.

'Your dad's good', I say. Everyone agrees that he is not.
Kurdish manners. They'd rather talk about the white walls
painted by everyone. It's taken two weeks
to see everything come up bright and agree on a carpet.

Above the fireplace, the painted woman cries.
A big-eyed horse looks over her left shoulder.
Beyond the white flicks of her tears, the mirror on her wall
reflects a minute in the Syrian street she watches:
the brush marks of soldiers drag her son away,
hands roped behind his back, black bag over his head.

Their country is an idea not shared by countries.
That is why the painted woman cries
as she stares out of the window at her son.
That is why an architect has time for painting,
time to take his younger boy to Nursery each day.
He says he'll make white sculptures as big as planes -
steel origami birds of hope, like the swans he draws.
He longs for white houses with no sharp angles -
giant garlic bulbs, like his grandfather's by the lake.

Everyone gets in the fifty pound car, even those in nightclothes.
We jolt over bumps to the house of a friend from Lebanon.
It's gone midnight. As we unload, curtains swish open.
Neighbours switch on lights, stare out of windows.

Lost Man

He hands me a painting light as a lampshade.
'It's lost child', he says, 'with only mum.
In this country, there many lost childs.'

The boy with red hair stares – hideously lost.

It's the kind of painting you'd do
the year the dragonflies didn't hatch
and the ice cream factory closed down.

It's almost the blue boy with one clear tear
you'd buy in a seaside shop
next to the novelty corkscrew.
It's almost a painting by numbers.

It's a gift.   What do I do with it?
It's by someone lost
who draws shepherds with guns.
He draws footprints
which stamp flowers into the mud.
He draws footprints
and invites children to fill them
with what's been stamped on in their lives.

The boy with red hair is looking for a wall.
He's lost, face down on the passenger seat.
I should find him a home - but not mine.

For Hulya
in memoriam

You come from stony tracks, from flights
on foot and plane to that shop turned house
with Ishmael, your football crazy twin.
I talk about 'the sun today' and school.

We meet at tables. I bring clay and colours
and draw a house for you, flat roofed, in rocks.
You scrawl it pink, a slab of Kurdish home
in Turkish peaks, then yellow - sunflowers.

You're small, straggly, smell like laundry
straight from tumble dry. Brain aged ten,
body much the same, but Ishmael says:
'She is twin. Hulya, me, we both fifteen.'

You grip a teaspoon handle in your fist,
scratch a flower of home, then another.
'Red and yellow. Many, many growing
by our houses there', says Ishmael.

He takes a knife and draws the sign
that magic men hang round horses' heads:
the triangle of luck, centred with a dot,
glued to children's heads, stuck on cows.

*

Another year and you'd have learnt
English words like 'red' and 'yellow'.

I hope you find a horse with wings:
dig your trainers tight into its flanks,
fly up to mountains, gallop into lakes.

Other people, other lives

7

Seven, a sacred number:
loaves and fishes
in the catacombs of Rome.

At the mouth of the Humber,
seven men from Somalia
lie on top of sliced coconuts:
dead at the end of a pier
in their container coffin.

Seven black faces: airless, ended
above white swans who feed on spilt grain –
chicken feed, not good enough for loaves.

Seven men who did not run across fields
chased by a helicopter,
who did not smell grain
or the pine stacks in the timber-yard;
who did not arrive at the local town
to have their blackness sneered at
by grey girls in the 'Top Nosh' café;
who did not walk to freedom or thumb a lift;
who lie still as the dead pigeon
by New Holland signal box.

Over the bridge, the korma eaters
wash down chicken and creamed coconut
with bottled beers from far-away.

Seven, a sacred number:
Did they say prayers together?

Did they talk of pigeons?

Walk/talk/mountain

'You'll need at least a litre of water',
says the guide, 'and butties for the top.'
The word 'butties' tells you she's English
but La Maroma is a Spanish mountain.

That was the day before. You need a guide
because there and back's an eight hour slog,
the clouds can come down quickly at the top
and the helicopter might not find you.

     *

Beyond the flat sand of the football field,
our boots bang off stones. Pine cones
lie at our feet, stripped to ragged cores
by the night fingers of pine martens.

'We'll keep the reservoir in the same place',
she says, 'so we can check our position.'
We look down on poly tunnels, imagine
box after box of watery tomatoes.

She bends, pinches the base of a calyx
and demonstrates the pop out tongue of toad flax.
The flytrap flick from the petalled mouth
leads to talk of sprung traps checked at dawn.
'We had a sheep farm in Wales', she says.
'You hold badgers down with a forked stick –
they're so angry before you let them go.
The foxes take over badgers' sets
and fill them with a mess of bones and feathers.'

On a high crag to the right, four wild deer.
They silhouette against the 9am sun
and jump from rock to rock. Their hoofs land
with the sound of waterdrops on dry soil.

The summit pulls us upwards, past grape hyacinths
whose purple beaded blooms suggest
specimens mounted on green sticks,
like the dyed brains of laboratory mice.

The clammy sweat of day-packs against our backs
means a welcome rest for oranges and water.
She sits on a mat which is mostly air,
says it's ideal for the concrete seats at the football
in November. She's keen, goes every week
and has switched her allegiance from Crewe to Malaga.

Far below, white diagrams of housing –
estates for foreigners who like flatness
and an easy drive to the sea and shops.

*

Our talk runs out when we sense the summit.
The rock slip needs hands as well as feet.
Deer droppings, like brown hailstones, mark the routes
which cross our clumsy drag up and up and up.
We spot black specks in the sky and guess vultures
until the crow's caw breaks the quiet.

Suddenly, the vertical groove runs out.
Our destination rears up before us
with a growl of cold, a sacred shout of rock
vaster than the cross of a cathedral floor.
She says, 'It's the size of four football fields.'

At the centre, a monument of cemented blocks
adds four metres to the height of La Maroma.
She takes the camera, snaps the photo of proof.
'Nirvana' and 'Kurt Cobain' in spray paint
prove that someone found the top of the world
hard to understand but of great personal value.

The thin air throbs with the summit stillness
of violent movement stopped. The snow capped tips
of the Sierra lull. Wave after grey-blue wave
of jagged crests fold into the distance.

*

Lunch is black rinded manchego cheese,
curd of ewe's milk which tastes of warm barns
crammed between slabs of bread, roughly cut,
followed by the home-made, sticky, heavy
marzipan fruitiness of Simnel cake.
Her healthy butty has more lettuce leaves in it
than the princess who felt the pea had mattresses.

On the far map of winding roads, red roofs
washed pink by distance, foothills splashed
with dark dots of holm oak,
blue squares of swimming pools,
bare oblongs of raisin drying beds and -
when we look with knowledge - battlefields,
fortresses, Arab cisterns, orchards of avocado,
minarets converted into bell towers,
groves of chirimoya - the custard apple.

As walkers do, we talk about boots.
She says, 'Flesh and green were last year's colours
in Chamonix in nineteen eighty-nine
so this pair of suede was pretty cheap.
Of course, the colour's gone over the years.'
She is interested in my scuffed Clarks,
which have survived rats and drains in Asia
and the leg gorging peat bogs of the Dales.

*

Then we dive, feet first, over the edge,
begin the parabolic flight down,
trampoline off scree, the curve
of the fall taking us. In our rush of speed,
we mistake rusty lichen on rock outcrops
for red paint left by German walkers.

She stops. The reservoir is not in the same place.
She goes to a high place to read the bumps.
The river valley is too wide, different
and the juniper bushes are not there.
After ten minutes of free fall,
we're an hour out of direction.
      We criss-cross, switchback
towards the same view of the reservoir.

She sees a white village, where more children
speak German than Spanish at the school
and knows that we are where we should be,

New sure-footedness takes us quickly down.
Our hot hands fill with blood, fingers fat
and red. Our feet pulse with twinges of blisters.

We slow to the pace of flower spotting:
identify bunches of white alyssum,
the wild sort prized by apothecaries;
the marshmallow whites and pinks of candytuft
and the blow football seeds of the asphodel.

Ant lines cross our path, led by knowing guides.
We respect the minuteness of their journeys.
The track twists and turns, hairpin bends
past a broken circle of dry-stone wall:
a keep, a rocky pen for goats or sheep.
We talk about the roundness of pinfolds,
the circular beauty of enclosures
built to hold the fight of stray animals.
The buzz of a chain saw. One last swig
empties our water bottles. We fill our packs
with 'firelighters' – pine cones untouched by martens.

   *

How do you get by if you live here without money,
a foreigner alone in sunny Spain? In Cheshire,
she did youth work jobs on dump estates,
and supply teaching – her unusual combination
of French, PE and sex education was in demand.
'I'm sure I was a bit of a cow then', she says,
'but you had to be to get their respect.
I didn't know the rules, let the fifth year lads
run their own game. They taught me to referee.'

Now she follows the routes of goatherds,
devises short walks for rich pensioners,
takes in laundry, cleans houses, does bar work.

She lived out on the campo but hasn't had much luck
with husbands. The last hung himself in the window,
framed for close inspection 'with extras'.
The friend who found the body did not recover
and had to return to England for treatment.

You can walk your problems away, they say.
We walk. Can you walk a lump off your breast
or walk away twenty years of marriage?
We walk. It's for the walker to decide, becoming familiar
with Axarquia, which routes to take, when to join
another or when to leave the route in search
of new sights. We walk. We walk off the mountain.

*

Back at the bar, baldy with the earring asks,
'Up there, did you see any, you know, creatures?'

We down a glass of Tuborg and a glass of 'clara'.
It's late afternoon – the sound of goat bells drifts in.

She says, 'There was nothing to go back for.
I've got good friends here. I enjoy the football.'

On the train near the farm where Joseph Bramah, pioneer of hydraulic engineering, grew up.

Everything's wet, everything drips at Penistone -
even the greenhouse where the blur of a man pots up plants,
even the pub signs and the piles of chemical drums.

You'd enjoy the continuous flow.

Round here, you dammed the brooks.
As you kicked the twigs and mud apart,
the sudden rush of water
started thoughts in your head
which ended up as large and small cylinders
filled with liquid, fitted with pistons, connected with a pipe,
lifting heavy objects from floor to floor.

You were like that boy who stayed behind after school
to look at sun spots through a home-made telescope
and got a job at NASA, making maps of Mars,
except you were a bird scarer, a farm lad.
Yokes and wooden wheels were your everyday.

You'd love the flush of the toilet on this train.
You'd listen to the ticking of small parts between carriages,
thrill at the onrush of breath as the automatic door opens.
You'd find out the workings of these objects – the science.

You were born before the iron horse,
long before the girl opposite who shouts,
"She's had all her hair chopped off.'

You'd notice the parallel tracks of tractor tyres
which smear the fields like vaseline.
You'd sit with your case with its unpickable brass locks,
amazed at the clean smells and shoulder bags.

There's no hunger now, Joseph, no danger of famine,
no pressure to leave this underwater land
for the night soiled back alleys of London

The air is full of waves.

Wife

He ruts home, wants something – skin, slit – somewhere
to shove his fist or his prick, kicks open our lump of a door,
heaves in, flails like his jacket on the line outside.
So I hide in 'OK' among Corrie babes in cling film black,
hope he's not real, not there, won't say, *Where's me tea,
bitch!* But I trap his eye, catch the roar inside felt
from way back, take in his slack mouthed, *Tea, bitch!*
and, before feathers and fur fly on the fifth floor, think:

I've had mine, four cheese pizza: parmesan, ricotta -
those Italian words which mean a farm on a hillside,
granny nips the kiddies' cheeks, a meal outside,
heat, everyone happy inside. Family, care.
Then he grabs my hair. *Geroff that chair. Gerupstairs.*
Already miles from home. Already pulling off his belt.

Teenage son

Mam, have ye bin doon the park playin' cricket?
Ye've caught a skyer of me dad, like Dinger's
last week. We gorrus a new baal like, champion,
reed as a bliddy neb, dropped doon in his eye.
He gorra reet shiner, Ribena colour like.
A lass cud've held it – it wor that pipsy!
His sister had to gan doon the precinct
an' buy a packet o' frozen peas to clag on.

Eee, mam, it's serious. Divn't cry, mam.
Aa gorra setificate for me art today,
for me drawin' of yor jewellery box.
Ye na, the one wi the spinnin' ballerina,
maeks a soond like a bord wi tonsillitis.
Aa give it a cloot but aa cudn't fettle her.

999

Forearms turned upwards.
Stiff long fingers, shaking
like a fairground generator.

Scratches:
the landlady's cat's been at your wrists.

Blood
like the dark drops of a hare's slit throat
splashing in a white basin.

Sounds:
a calf bellows in the corner of a lorry.

Punk brought out the pain in you,
the stiffs still stacked up in your head
from your holiday job
as a hospital porter.
You wanted to damage
your trolley pushing hands.

You'd been getting ready,
shoved metal in your ears,
hurled yourself up and down,
banged your head on ceilings,
pushed nails up your nose.
God that must have hurt.

You hacked at yourself
but didn't change the blade
of your Stanley knife –
it was a rough job.

God it must have hurt, Catholic boy –
your bungled stigmata.

I ran your wrists under the cold tap,
tore up your shirt, bound you.
I saw the shallowness of your shout.
You didn't use something sharp.
You didn't stay in your own room.

Five boards waiting

It's true, the simplest things
last, like trades or undone business.

We'd been talking wood, the linen boxes,
how wood becomes jewels and miracles
when all the trees are gone, how wood is
hidden in the blood, how wood is a dance.

There'd been a catalogue of deaths:
the end of piano duets, a coma in Crete,
a slip from a cliff rope, two cancers.

*

Five boards, he said. *Five boards –
I sent them to the wheelwright Chipping Norton way,
told him to use copper nails. That way I'll last longer.*

He'd stepped out of 'The Norman Knight'
the day before the dance, on his way to ninety,
curry sauce stains on his shirt of old man blue,
drips in his white beard, goose grass on his cuff
but still sharp, still the thing we're all after.

*I've had the best crop of wheat ever so I sent
five boards – one extra, just in case.
It's thirty years since I cut down the oak.
It was in the way. You couldn't do that now.*

I knew him as a singer first, farmer second.
I knew him when he told his wife to scarper,
took up with his secretary, kept things tax efficient.

I'm still a working farmer, born in those trees.
I've built my land piece by piece. My grandad
was a farm worker. I'm worth three million,
still a working farmer, so no inheritance tax.

A man in both sheep and arable, a hare
who can see what lies around the bend.

I'd like, he said, *some nice requiems.*
I'd like, he said, *some Handel or Verdi:*
there's plenty of money in the kitty.

Wool from these hills was carried
to the high, rose cities of Italy. The woolpacks
carried jewels and miracles, the thing
they were all after, the Gloucester fleece.

It was, he said, *the softest in the world.*
It was, he said, *the gold that built the churches,*
the gold which bought the merchants of Campden
some nice requiems.

He's off to America, to stay with a daughter

I'll get my fiddle down from the loft.
I've got cats for strings, a horse for the bow.
I'll play a tune, fiddle my way towards those
five boards. Tomorrow, I'll dance on the Green.

He has no undone business to speak of.